Miklós Rózsa

Sonata per Flauto Solo

Op. 39

(1983)

Faber Music Limited

London

© 1986 by Faber Music Ltd
First published in 1986 by Faber Music Ltd
3 Queen Square London WC1N 3AU
Music drawn by Lincoln Castle Music
Cover design by M & S Tucker
Printed in England by Caligraving Ltd

Duration: c. 16 minutes

Miklós Rózsa was born in Budapest in 1907 and as a boy came into direct contact with the authentic music of the Hungarian peasantry which was to leave an indelible imprint on his own compositions: no doubt the fact that folksong is in its pristine state monodic, unharmonized, helps explain the success of his work for unaccompanied instruments – the Sonata for two violins (1933), the popular Clarinet Sonatina (1951) and the present work, composed in the winter of 1983. Rózsa did not, however, remain in Hungary; feeling the need of a wider context in which to develop he studied at the Leipzig Conservatory and lived successively in London and Paris before settling in Hollywood in 1940, whence his film music quickly won him international renown. Among his concert works the *Theme, Variations and Finale* (1933), the *Concerto for Strings* (1943), the Piano Sonata (1948), the 1953 Violin Concerto (written for, and first performed and recorded by, Jascha Heifetz) and the 1979 Viola Concerto are outstanding. His autobiography *Double Life* was published in London and New York in 1982.

The help of Jonathan Snowden, of the London Philharmonic Orchestra, in editing the text of this work for publication, is gratefully acknowledged. The Sonata was first performed on 1 December 1984 by Bonita Boyd under the auspices of the California Chamber Symphony Society at Pepperdine University.

Christopher Palmer

For Christopher Palmer

Sonata per Flauto Solo

Miklós Rózsa
Op.39

I

*May be played *normale* if preferred.

6

II

Andante, quasi pastorale (♩=ca.60)

Più animato (♩=ca.120)

V.S.

III

V.S.